Anne Bradstreet

by Phoebe Besbekis

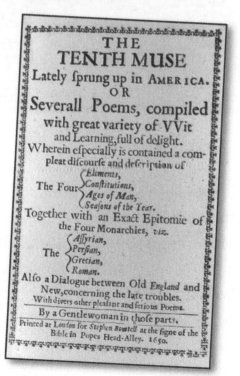

THE
TENTH MUSE
Lately sprung up in AMERICA.
OR
Severall Poems, compiled
with great variety of VVit
and Learning, full of delight.
Wherein especially is contained a com-
pleat discourse and description of
The Four { Elements,
Constitutions,
Ages of Man,
Seasons of the Year.
Together with an Exact Epitomie of
the Four Monarchies, viz.
The { Assyrian,
Persian,
Grecian,
Roman.
Also a Dialogue between Old England and
New, concerning the late troubles.
With divers other pleasant and serious Poems.
By a Gentlewoman in those parts.
Printed at London for Stephen Bowtell at the signe of the
Bible in Popes Head-Alley. 1650.

HOUGHTON MIFFLIN   BOSTON

In 1650, a book of poems was published in London. The small book was notable for two reasons. It was the first book of poems published in English by a woman. More important, it was the first poetry written by a person living in a North American colony.

The woman was Anne Bradstreet. She lived in the Massachusetts Bay Colony in the 1600s. Anne was born in England around 1612. She was a Puritan. Puritans were the people who sailed on the *Mayflower*. You may know the Puritans as "Pilgrims." They held the first Thanksgiving.

England treated the Puritans badly They came to the New World so that they could practice their religion in peace. They settled Plymouth in 1620. Anne and her husband, Simon, arrived 10 years later.

Anne and her family probably lived in a house like the one in the photo above of Pilgrim Village at Plimoth Plantation in Plymouth, Massachusetts. The village is a replica of the colony as it was in Anne's time.

Anne's father and husband were important Puritan men. Each became governor of the Bay Colony. Anne, however, is the member of the family that most people remember best.

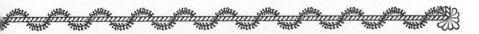

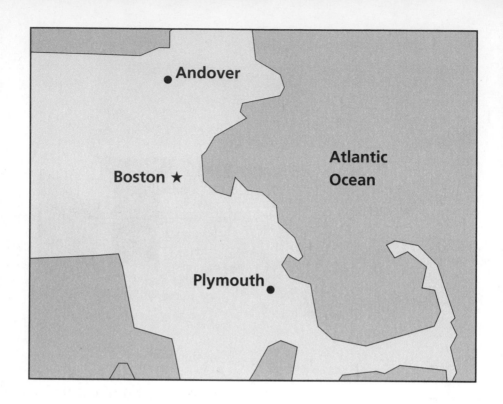

Around 1640, Anne moved to Andover, Massachusetts. She spent the rest of her life in the small village. She raised her eight children there. She wrote poems about her life and her family.

Anne had a mission as a poet. She wanted to describe daily life in the wilderness of the new colony. She proved that the New World could have its own literature. Her simple poems left a heritage of writing.

Anne Bradstreet wrote simple, beautiful poems. She wrote about the births of her four boys and four girls. She told how she missed her husband when he was away. She wrote about her sadness when her grandchildren died.

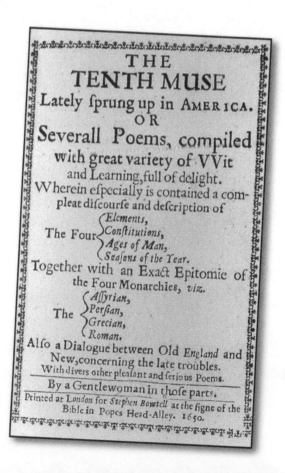

THE
TENTH MUSE
Lately fprung up in AMERICA.
OR
Severall Poems, compiled
with great variety of VVit
and Learning, full of delight.
Wherein efpecially is contained a com-
pleat difcourfe and defcription of
The Four { Elements,
Conftitutions,
Ages of Man,
Seafons of the Year.
Together with an Exact Epitomie of
the Four Monarchies, viz.
The { Affyrian,
Perfian,
Grecian,
Roman.
Alfo a Dialogue between Old England and
New, concerning the late troubles.
With divers other pleafant and ferious Poems.
By a Gentlewoman in thofe parts.
Printed at London for Stephen Bowtell at the figne of the
Bible in Popes Head-Alley. 1650.

Ine poem was about how she felt when her house burned. In that poem, Anne told about the loss of important items. She loved many of the things she lost. She mentioned a table where people sat for dinner. She talked about the chest that held tablecloths. The reader can feel how deeply sad Anne was to have lost her things. One of the lost items might have been a cradle like the one in the photo.

But Anne's poetry had a deeper meaning. Like all Puritans, Anne was very religious. The burning of the house was a symbol of the things she owned. She felt that we should not worry about things. Instead, we should care about the people we love and our religion.

Life in the colonies could be hard. Anne probably had much work to fill her day. She must have loved writing, however, because she found the time to do it.

Anne never wanted her poems published. Her first book of poems was published without her knowledge. One of her relatives published it in London without asking Anne. Her second book of poetry wasn't published until six years after she died in 1672. Many people today like that book the best of all her works.

Now, more than 300 years later, Anne might be surprised to know that we still read her poetry. We think about and value what she had to say about life in the colonies.